Ants

by Grace Hansen

ABDO
INSECTS
Kids

Visit us at www.abdopublishing.com

Published by Abdo Kids, a division of ABDO, P.O. Box 398166, Minneapolis, Minnesota 55439.

Copyright © 2015 by Abdo Consulting Group, Inc. International copyrights reserved in all countries. No part of this book may be reproduced in any form without written permission from the publisher.

Printed in the United States of America, North Mankato, Minnesota.

032014

092014

♻ PRINTED ON RECYCLED PAPER

Photo Credits: Shutterstock, Thinkstock

Production Contributors: Teddy Borth, Jennie Forsberg, Grace Hansen

Design Contributors: Dorothy Toth, Renée LaViolette, Laura Rask

Library of Congress Control Number: 2013952088

Cataloging-in-Publication Data

Hansen, Grace.

 Ants / Grace Hansen.

   p. cm. -- (Insects)

ISBN 978-1-62970-036-6 (lib. bdg.)

Includes bibliographical references and index.

1. Ants--Juvenile literature.   I. Title.

595.79--dc23

                2013952088

Table of Contents

Ants

Ants are insects. Butterflies, bees, and mosquitoes are insects too.

Ants live almost everywhere on Earth. Most ants live in **nests** in the ground.

Ants can be black, red, and brown. Ants can be yellow and green too.

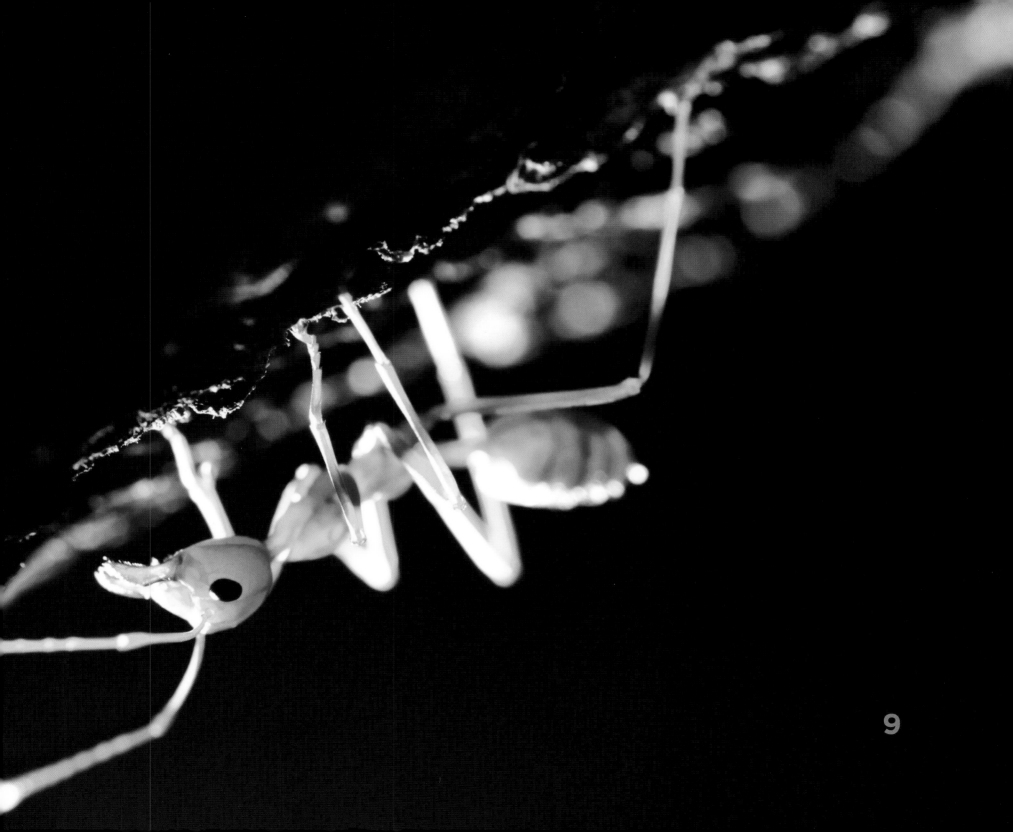

Ants have three main body parts. They are the head, **thorax**, and the **abdomen**.

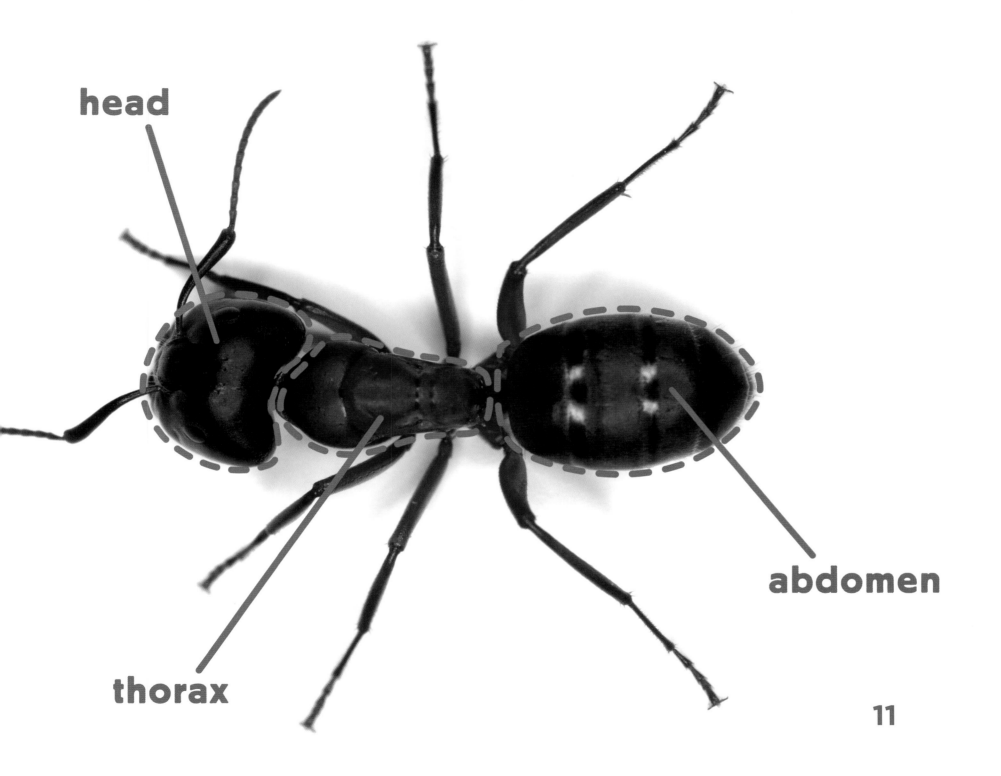

head

thorax

abdomen

11

An ant's head has two eyes,
a mouth, and two **antennae**.

13

Ants have six legs.

Some ants have wings.

15

Ant Colonies

Ants live together in a group called a **colony**. Each ant has an important job to do in the colony.

16

Ant **colonies** have three main members. They are the queen, female workers, and males.

queen

male

female
worker

19

Ants Help the Earth

Ants **protect** plants by
eating other insects. Their
underground homes keep
the soil healthy.

20

More Facts

- A queen ant can live for many years. In that time, she will lay millions of eggs.

- Ants use chemicals to communicate.

- If you weighed all of the ants in the world, they would be heavier than the total weight of all humans.

- Ants are very strong. They can lift up to 20 times their body weight!

Glossary

abdomen – the back part of an insect's body.

antennae – the two long, thin "feelers" on an insect's head.

colony – a group of animals of one kind living together.

nest – a home made by animals or insects to live or lay eggs.

protect – to guard against harm or danger.

thorax – the middle part of an insect's body.

Index

abdokids.com

Use this code to log on to abdokids.com and access crafts, games, videos and more!

Abdo Kids Code:
IAK0366